IMAGES OF WALES

RHONDDA
REVISITED

Contents

Acknowledgements

The authors wish to thank the following individuals and organisations for their considerable help in the compilation of this book. We are particularly indebted to Malcolm Saunders, Allan Jones, and Phillip John Davies who have willingly opened up their excellent photographic collections, thus allowing us to improve considerably our intended publication. We sincerely apologise to anyone who has helped us over the years if they have been inadvertently omitted from the following list: John Brown, Lynda Davies, Margaret Davies, Herbert Hunt, Graham Mundy, Annie May Jones, Cyril John, May Mitchell, Penpych Primary School, Julie Spiller, and the Penyrenglyn Project, Valley Kids Penygraig and our computer teachers Julie Meredith, Lesley Wilbourne, and Mark Gibbs, for making it possible to handle word processing and save us hours of work.

We would gratefully record our indebtedness to the many photographers whose work is featured in this book, some unknown and the following that have become synonymous with Rhondda: Albert Davies (Porth), Levi Ladd (Tonypandy), Stephen Timothy (Pentre), E. Lester (Treherbert), Marlin Norman (Pentre), D.J. Ryan (Treorchy), J. Johnson, Cyril Batstone (Pentre) and Ernest T. Bush.

Our special thanks go to the committee of Treherbert OAP Hall for the use of their hall, and last but not least, to our wives Doreen Jenkins and Mavis Green for their patience and understanding and to Ernie Fair for his excellent introduction.

Introduction

I feel very proud to have been asked to write an introduction to this new volume of Rhondda photographs, especially as an outsider! Well, not quite, it is now over sixty years since I, as a young lad of fifteen, came to the Rhondda from blitzed Swansea.

No stranger to the valleys in those days could claim, 'love at first sight', its mountains were scarred with coalmines and tips and its rivers ran black with coal dust. The winding streets of miner's cottages, so clean and neat inside, were mostly painted in dark colours to fit in with the environment.

But the Rhondda was not only its buildings and mountains, it was also the spirit of its people creating a close community in spite of all the odds against it, that spirit was exported together with its coal taking the name Rhondda Valley to all parts of the world.

Throughout my life in the Rhondda I have been closely associated with the local Methodist church, the old Wesleyan, and when, in 1987, the old building had to come down and the new one was built I compiled a book in celebration of the event called Hymns and Hard Work. The title referred to the Methodist Church but it could equally have applied to the Rhondda.

But olden times were not just about hard work and tribulations, there was also much joy and laughter too, we had cinemas, music, drama, carnivals, sport, brass bands, eisteddfods, dance halls, chapels and Sunday schools – and the Sunday school outing was one of the highlights of the year, sometimes to Barry and Porthcawl, but more often through the tunnel to Aberavon. Those outings contained all the adventures of a child's dream, the journey that seemed to go on and on, the miles and miles of sand, the ladies in their big hats and umbrellas to guard against sun or rain, and what seemed to be the 'feeding of the five thousand' within minutes of arriving. And to think there were once 151 Non-Conformist churches and their Sunday schools in the Rhondda with over 85,000 worshippers.

Every district seems to have its miner's institutes, the Rhondda had at one time twenty-one of them, these imposing buildings were centres of social life (as were the chapels), but also provided a place of learning and discussion for many. The miner's institutes, with their great libraries, played a big part in the creation of our present public libraries.

The music and amateur dramatics of bygone days were the foundations that brought national and international recognition to our brass bands, our choirs and our dramatic societies.

Try playing the game 'I remember when' as I often do and let the photographs of this book help you along. Remember the dozens of double-decker buses taking the workers to Alfred Polikoff's, the local derby matches between Treherbert and Treorchy and many other places in the valley, which were held at Christmas time, the carnival bands in all their bright colours, the Saturday matinee, the courting days with walks along the mountain 'new roads', the Bracchis, the Red and White long-distance buses. Relive those days again through the pages of this book. I have a special memory playing as a young sixteen-year-old drummer with the E.V. Davies band at the Lido (Tynewydd Labour Club).

My congratulations to Emrys Jenkins and Roy Green for stimulating our memories and reminding us of days gone by and for bringing together so many photographs and so much information.

And as for the famous line – 'I came, I saw, I conquered', well, I was conquered, and I stayed.

Ernie Fair
July 2004

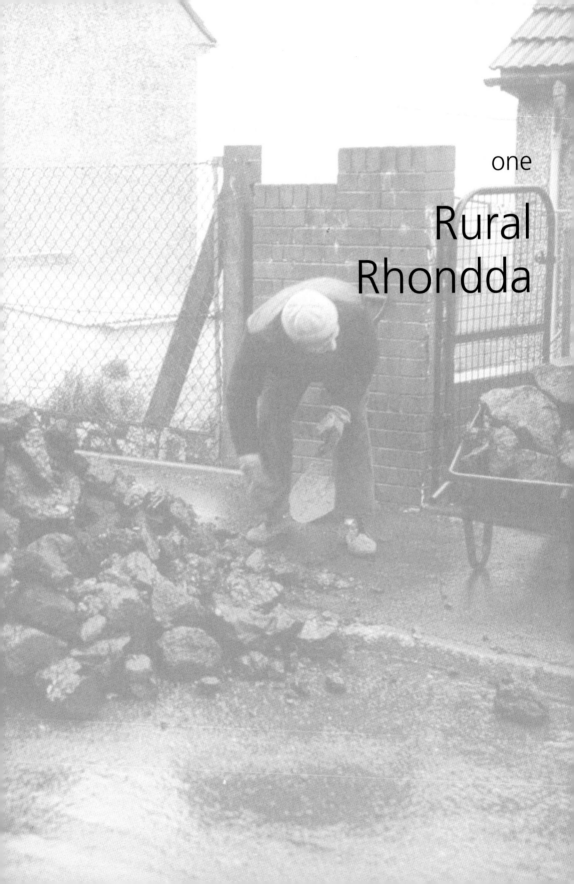

one

Rural
Rhondda

A view of Treorchy, *c.* 1902. Note the number of streets and buildings yet to be built.

A view of Brittania and Llwyncelyn, *c.* 1904.

Brynheulog House, Carne Street, Pentre around 1912 showing the home of Mr and Mrs E.H. Davies.

Mountain View, formerly Bulls Row, Tynewydd, *c.* 1953. The oak tree is a landmark and is documented on old Ordanance Survey maps.

Clyngwyn Farm, *c.* 1925. Standing on the right can be seen farmer William Jenkins and the man on the left is Will Page.

Darren Park Lake, Ferndale, *c.* 1923.

East Road and Edmund Street, Tylorstown. A branch of the Mid-Rhondda Co-operative Society is on the right. Top left is the Holy Trinity church, which was erected in 1883 at a cost of £1,400.

Rhondda Transport bus in Llwynypia Road, 1980. The gasometer (the round building in the centre of the photograph) was demolished in 1998 and the building on the left was demolished in 1999 to make way for a McDonald's restaurant. The building on the left is the Glamorgan (Scotch) Colliery Power House played a big part in the Tonypandy riots in 1910. The building was protected by a handful of officials and police to prevent the strikers taking the Power House and flooding the mine.

A general view of Treorchy, *c.* 1900. Note that there is no cinema attached to the Park and Dare and that Dyfodwg Street and Illtyd Street have yet to be built. On the left is Glyncoli Colliery.

A view of Treorchy, *c.* 1936.

Maerdy Railway Station, *c.* 1908. The end of the line of the Taff Vale Railway was in Rhondda Fach.

Treorchy Park, *c.* 1935. Note the Gorsedd circle in the field.

Pentre viewed from the Maendy Croft, 1925.

MOUNTAIN VIEW OF RESEVOIR & BLAENCWM, TREHERBERT 8260

A mountain view of the reservoir at Blaencwm, *c.* 1945.

The site of Treherbert Park, *c.* 1900. Bute Colliery and Bute cottages are on the left.

Strand and Rhondda Road, Ferndale.

The Strand and Rhondda Road, Ferndale, *c.* 1920. At No. 7, Strand was Hodge's, clothier; No. 4, David Hughes, butcher and No. 6 Lipton Ltd, grocer.

The Homes.   Llwynypia.

Llwynypia Homes for the poor and destitute was taken over by the health authority as a hospital and it was agreed that all residents could stay for the rest of their lives. The last resident was Chris Jordan who died in 1986.

A view of Ton Pentre with Maendy Colliery in the background.

Treherbert and Penyrenglyn, St Mary's church and Ynysofeio tip.

A view of Ferndale, *c.* 1918.

A view of Pontygwaith showing the railway station on the right from around 1937.

A view of Porth, *c.* 1902.

Pentre and Treorchy, *c.* 1904.

A general view of Pentre, *c.* 1950. Note the prefabricated houses that were built after the war, in order to relieve the housing shortage.

Gorsedd Stones and Eisteddfod Pavilion 1928.

Penpych Blaencwm, *c.* 1935. Glenrhondda Colliery (Hook and Eye) can be seen in the background.

A general view of Treorchy, c. 1905. Cemetery Road is in the foreground with Stuart Street in the centre of the picture. Note the two stonemason's yards on opposite sides and also the trucks crossing Cemetery Road.

Cardiff Street, Treorchy is in the centre of the picture and is seen here leading on to Cemetery Road. Note the condition of the roads in the side streets and also that Gosen Chapel can be seen to the left in this scene.

House coal is being delivered to the home of a colliery workman, which sometimes had to be carried through the house to the coal *cwtch* (shed).

A view of Pentre from Ystrad. Maendy Hall can just be seen poking out over the top of the trees.

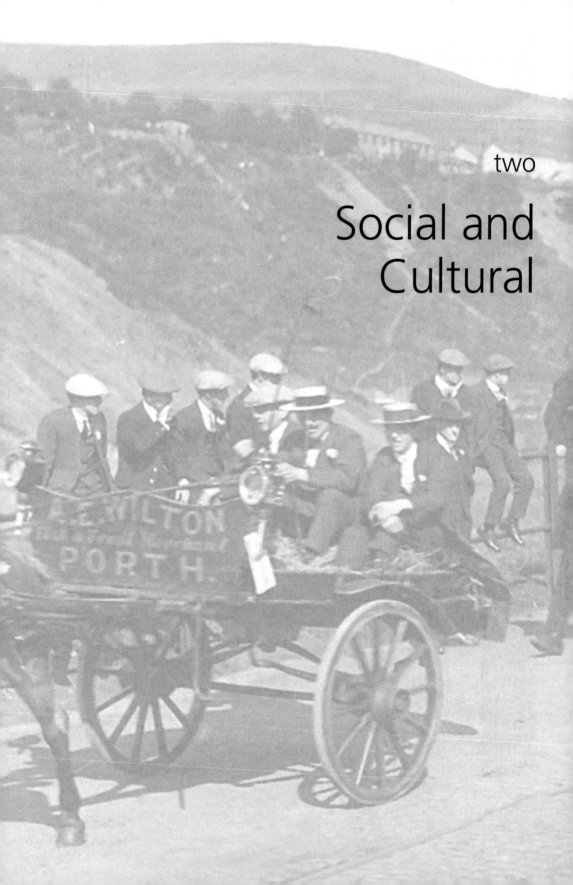

two

Social and
Cultural

Dolly's Wedding, 1925. From left to right, back row: Mr Jones, Ben Mundy, Lillian Annie Constance Dayment, Fred Jones, Jean Jones, Albert Lang and Sam Dayment. Front row: Mrs Jones, Jacob Stanley Jones, Dolly Jones (née Dayment) and Mrs Dayment.

The Wedding of Mr T.S. Gibbons and Miss A. Harris, July 1930. They were both staff members of the Rhondda Education Authority and Mr Gibson was the Hon. Secretary of the Ton Pentre Golf Club.

Sunday school carnival float from early in the twentieth century.

Cwmni Drama Bethlehem (Bethlehem Drama Company) MC Porth 1923-24.

The Mayor of Rhondda (Alderman Joe Lewis) has a chat with Miss Gordon Phillips (Patron of
Treherbert Canine Society) at a four-class dog show held at Treherbert in 1959. Miss Phillips is from
Treorchy.

The Mayoress of the Rhondda (Mrs J. Lewis) welcomes Air Chief Marshal Sir Hugh Pugh Lloyd, GBE, KCB, MC, DFC, DLLD, to the Porth RAFA Club where Sir Hugh was officially opening the club in September 1959.

Dewi Sant, Tonypandy garden party, 16 July 1914.

Treherbert Hospital Queen, 1933. From left to right: May Harding (Queen),-?-, Miss Williams, Miss Jones, Elsie Roberts, Sally Vaughan, Betty Argust and Marion Cassam.

Porth carnival, 1914.

The Primitive Methodist Sunday school teachers from Llwynypia, Whit Monday, 1914.

Ready for the Wales v Scotland rugby international in 1949. From left to right, back row: Ken Carroll, Harry Pearce, Dick Broome, John Morgan and Dai Morgan. Front row: Cliff Williams, Ivor Collins, Haydn Parfitt and George Thorner.

The Richards family living in No. 73 Blaencwm Terrace, 1910. From left to right, back row: Jack, Stanley, William, David and Eunice. Front row: Jane, Evan, Ellen, Margaret (mother), Morgan (father) with Elfed on his lap and –?–.

The Famous Neuralgia Band, 1917. On the left back row: Ben Mundy, and five unknowns. From left to right, front row: Tom Lewis, Frank Pegler, Tom Hibbs, -?- and -?-. Most of them worked on the Taff Vale Railway and were all staunch members of Emanuel Chapel, Station Street, Treherbert.

Neuralgia Comic Band, 1920. On the left is Tom Hibbs, the girl is Lucy Travis (*née* Pegler) and on the right, with the clothes horse and bottles, is Ben Mundy. I wonder if their signature tune was 'I know a song that gets on your nerves, gets on your nerves'.

A concert in 1946/47 at Bethany Chapel, Treherbert. From left to right: Ceinwen Howells, Marion Haddrell, Blodwen Davies and Marion Llewellyn.

Treherbert Urdd Group 1937. From left to right: June Howard, Glenys Davies, Margaret Phillips, Eirona Phillips (Nona), Mair Cole, Nina Evans, Audrey Pegler and Ruth Waters. In front: Joy Thomas and Annette Howard.

Above left: Morgan Price shows off the latest fashion dressed in plus fours around 1920.

Above right: David Evans and friends show off their Sunday best for the camera. Pentre around 1910.

Tydraw Colliery officials and their wives enjoy a night out around 1950. Clockwise, from left: -?-, Mrs Thompson, Eileen Lewis, Lil King, Rene Rees, Trevor King, -?-, Jack Rees, Mavis Green, Roy Green, Mr Thompson and Elfed Lewis.

Potato-picking in Truro, Cornwall, *c.* 1950. These men, who all worked at Fernhill Colliery, were using their holidays from the mine to pick potatoes. From left to right, back row: Don Bundock, Harry Pearce and Dick Broome. Front row: Haydn Parfitt, Dai Morgan, Chalsey Hayward, -?- and Bram Jenkins.

Opposite below: The Volunteer Street Silver Jubilee Party, May 1935. Among those pictured are: twins Doreen and Doris Williams, Mary Barnet, Dennis Barnet, Elizabeth Thomas, Sylvia Owen, Mavis Owen, Rhianon Jones, Phyllis Roach, Joan Coles, Pamela Pumford, Gwyn Pumford, Jenny Evans and Mair Hughes.

Above: Fernhill Workmen are seen here at the last Presentation Supper held in the Blaenrhondda (Top) Club, on the closure of the colliery in 1981. From left to right, back row: Cyril Jones, Alan Evans, Haydn Stevens, Tess George, Myrddin James, Ken Carroll, Tom Mumford, Albert Clatworthy, -?- and Jack Barnes. Second row: Jack Wilkins, Dai Adams, -?- , Ron Thomas, Edwin Lewis, Jim Marsh, Bert Sealey, Dai Davies, Stan Ferguson, Myrddin (Muff) Thomas, Norman Spencer, Mel Grant, Dick Broome, Plennydd Jackson, Dixie Adams, Russ Thomas, Ron Morris and Idwal Llewellyn. Front row: Gillie Edwards, George Baker, Harry Pearce, George Rees, Don Bundock, Emlyn Jenkins, Cliff True, Dai Francis and Ron Griffiths.

Wesleyan Chapel, Treherbert, 50/50 Club Members, *c.* 1950. From left to right, back row: Dennis Coles, Donald Rees, Chrissie Fair, Trevor Davies, David O'Leary, Charlie Goodman, Bill Davies, David Ellis, Pauline Harris and Alun Parry. Second row: Joan Evans, ? Coles, Joyce Svendsen, Agnes Parsons, Betty Pritchard, Mair Evans, Evelyn Case, Eirwen Davies, Glenys Evans, Freda Rees and Wilf Harris. Third row: Jim and Dora Phelps (founders of the club), Roy Green, Muriel Case, Ernie Fair, Jimmy Lloyd, Winnie Harris, Gerald Harris, Brenda Rees and Wendy Phelps. Front row: Betty Richards, Tom Phelps, Cora Evans, Dilys Cousins, ? Cousins, John O'Leary and Colleen Harris.

three

Transport
and Trade

A Rhondda father and daughter pose with their cycles in around 1915.

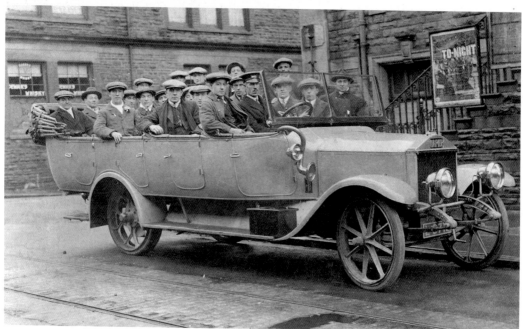

Rhondda Fach charabanc trip, probably to the races. Note the external horn and solid tyres.

A horse and trap in, *c.* 1910. A poster of the Palace cinema can be seen displayed in the butcher's window.

Wyndham Lewis, landlord of the Lion Hotel, High Street, Treorchy is seen here driving his Renault car in 1927. Gordon Rees is the boy in the background, Annie Rees sits in the back seat, and on her right are Roma Lewis and Norma Rees.

Rhondda Transport employees admire the Morris Cowley open-top car driven by the Rhondda transport inspector who is seen here around 1930.

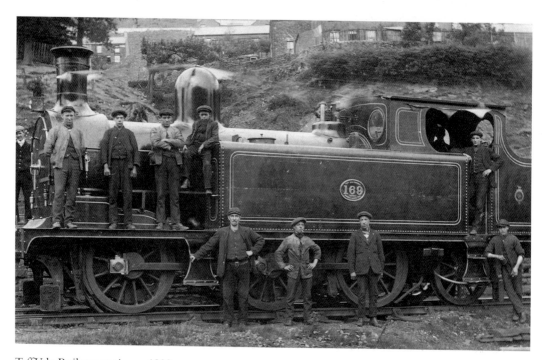

Taff Vale Railway engine, *c.* 1900.

Ystradyfodwg Fire Brigade with their Merryweather fire engine outside council offices Llewellyn Street, Pentre around 1890.

The Royal train at Porth Railway Station, 27 June 1912. During the visit of King George V and Queen Mary to Dinas Rescue Station and Treherbert.

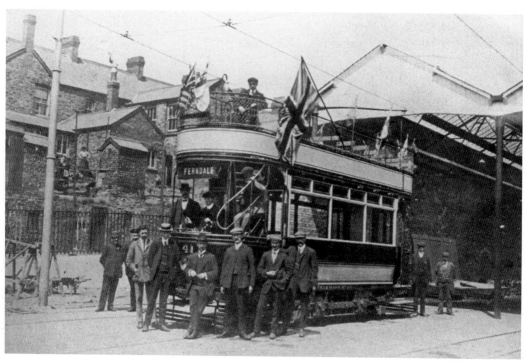

The first Rhondda tramcar to leave the depot went into service on 2 September 1908 and the driver was Mr C.W. Furness (representative of the consulting engineer). On the steps is Mr C.E.N. Gardner (overhead constructional engineer) and from left to right: Messrs H. Kinder, G.E. Roddy (Traffic Manager), T. Hopper (chief assistant-engineer), H.J. Nesbitt (general manager), A.E. Rolfe, (accountant), H.D. Johnstone (constructional engineer) and P.F. Stewart (assistant constructional engineer). At the rear is Mr J. James (overhead linesman).

On 1 February 1934, Mr T.G. Richardson (general manager of the Rhondda Tram-ways Co.) can be seen here driving the last car (No. 41) into the depot before the trams were substituted by modern omnibuses. This car was also the first to leave the depot in 1908, but it had been reconditioned at this time. The photograph shows Mr A.E. Rolfe (accountant) on the steps and from left to right, front row: Mr A.G. Slee (works superintendent), Mr F. Fortt (traffic manager), Mr H.M. Welch and J. Gibbons (two of the original employees, and chairman and secretary of the Rhondda Tramways Branch of the National General Union of Workers). As the tram ran into the depot a huge crowd sang 'Farewell, my own true love'.

A passenger train on the Rhondda-Swansea Bay railway line is about to enter the tunnel on the Blaencwm side.

Engine 4577, was pulling a Porth train to Maerdy, 15 February 1958.

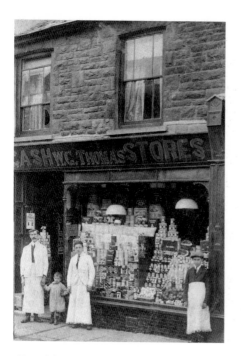

Above left: W.C. Thomas' Stores, Ferndale.

Above right: Robert Evans' Stores, Ferndale.

D. Roberts' Store, Maerdy.

Well-known shopkeeper H. Powell at Garfield House, Treherbert, *c.* 1910.

India and China Tea Co.'s shop on the corner of King Street, Ferndale.

Morris Ten, owned by Hendersons Coaches, Penygraig, 20 April 1979.

Sharpe Bros, Treorchy fruit and vegetable traders.

The Rhondda Valley Brewery lorry, *c.* 1915. Note the chain drive and solid tyres.

Pentre post office, Ystrad Road, *c.* 1910.

Michael Davies, undertaker, Station Street, Treherbert.

Michael Davies and hearse can be seen in his yard behind the rear of Emanuel Chapel, Station Street, Treherbert, around 1910.

Michael Davies' landau. The driver was known as 'Spencer the Cockney' as he originally came from London. The horses' names are Tommy and Prince.

Courage Brewery take over the ownership of the Marquis of Bute pub in Treherbert, 11 May 1988. Gwyn Rees, Rhondda Borough Council Mayor, is in the dray.

The last diesel trains to cross in Ystrad station on 28 March 1981, before the single line was introduced on 30 March 1981.

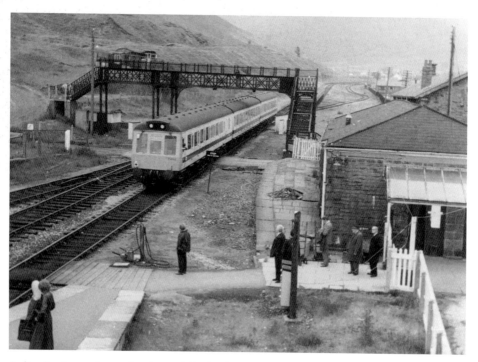

A diesel train, passing under the steel footbridge, arriving in Treherbert Station to pick up passengers for the return to Cardiff, 5 July 1978. The Revd Jeffrey Long is standing on the extreme right.

Treorchy Co-operative stores, *c.* 1975.

Thomas and Evans', Welsh Hills pop works (Corona), Porth, *c.* 1979. The works have now become a successful recording studio.

A Thomas and Evans' advertisement proclaiming, 'original Welsh Hills aerated waters' and picturing some of the bottles they used.

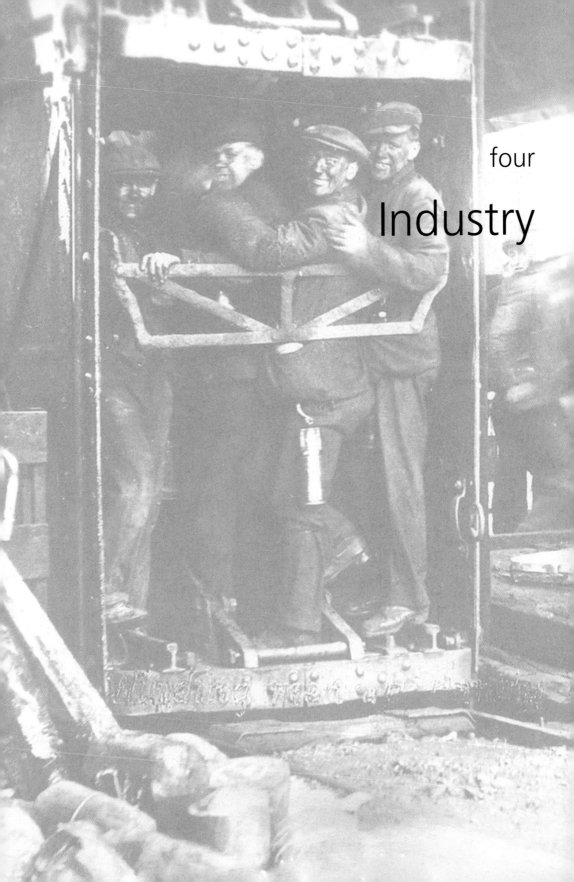

four

Industry

Fernhill Colliery, *c*. 1955.

Officials from Fernhill Colliery, Blaenrhondda from the early twentieth century.

Morlais Evans, on the left and Dick Rees, in the sawmill are seen here on the pit top of No. 3 shaft, Fernhill Colliery, Blaenrhondda, around 1965.

Fernhill Colliery showing No. 1 and No. 2 shafts. On the left is the colliery office with Office Row adjacent. One of the residents of Office Row stated that the colliers used to queue for their pay alongside the wall next to her garden. Her toilet was halfway up the garden, which meant that she would have to pass the men to use the toilet and felt embarrassed, as they would call out to her. She claimed that on pay day she never went to the toilet.

Bringing in the harvest, Tydraw Farm, Tynewydd, *c.* 1920.

Bute Colliery, Cwmsaebran Treherbert , was the first steam coal colliery to be sunk in the Rhondda in 1851, by W.S. Clarke, for the trustees of the Bute Estate, around 1920.

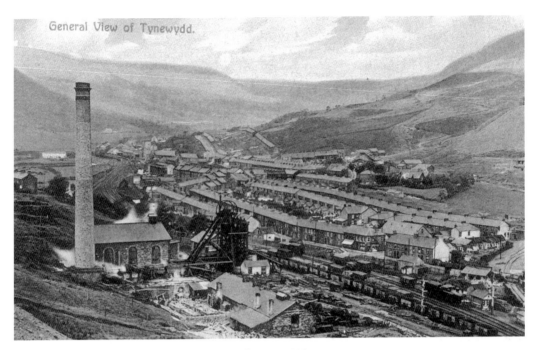

A general view of Tynewydd and Bute Colliery, *c.* 1910.

Great Western Collieries, Trehafod, *c.* 1936.

Ynysofeio Colliery, *c.* 1900.

Dare Colliery, Cwmparc, *c.* 1900.

Standard Colliery, Ynyshir, 1904 with the Wattstown United National Colliery at the rear on the right

Wattstown United National Colliery, c. 1915.

Maendy Colliery, Ton Pentre, *c.* 1904.

Pentre Colliery, *c.* 1902.

The pit bottom of the No. 5 shaft at Fernhill Colliery, Blaenrhondda in 1978.

Above left: Colliers ascending Pandy pit.

Above right: Pwllyrhebog signal box, situated on the 'up side' opposite Tonypandy goods station. The box controlled the section between Llwynypia Lower and Naval Colliery, also the incline to Blaenclydach and Cambrian Colliery (TaffVale), around 1920.

Workmen in the wagon repair sheds of the Ocean Coal Co., Cwmparc. From left to right, back row: David Jones, Orlando Jones, Eddy Rowe, Gwilym Morgan, Frankie Lloyd, John Haydn, Will Lloyd, Emir Jones, George Stephens, Jacky Morgan and Arthur Richardson. Middle row: David Perkins, Howard Williams, Ken Hughes, Dave Price, John Davies, Dick Griffiths, Emlyn Thomas, Jack Bowen, Cliff White, Don Morris and Cyril Cummings. Front row: Bob Peake, Roy Carter, Dave Thomas, Glyn Wigley, Rhys Morgan Rees, Johnny Roberts (behind Mr Rees), Johnny Gronow, Ivor Owen and Eirlydd Wright.

Tynybedw Colliery, Treorchy, *c.* 19004.

The winding-engine house for the No. 3 shaft, which housed a Leigh winding engine at Fernhill Colliery, Blaenrhondda seen here around 1965.

Parc Colliery, Cwmparc, Rescue Team, 1967. From left to right, back row: Alwyn Jones, Roy Harris and Dilwyn Butler. Front row: Brian Dee, E. Evans, Islwyn Morgan and Dai Chislett.

Cambrian Colliery and Llwyn Onn, Clydach Vale, *c.* 1908.

Glamorgan Colliery, Llwynypia, *c.* 1908.

The New Factory, Ynyswen

Alfred Polikoff's Factory, Treorchy. At the beginning of 1937 Lord Nuffield placed a great sum of money in trust for the purpose of assisting the government in their plans for the establishment of new industries in distressed areas; the Rhondda Valley was among them. With the cooperation of Mr Alfred Polikoff, and by 1939, a fine, modern factory was erected at Ynyswen, Treorchy. It covered some 80,000 square feet and was planned to accommodate over 1,500 work people. Production commenced on 6 March 1939, manufacturing boy's, youth's and men's outerwear in the tailoring section. The dress section produced stylish dresses and blouses for ladies. During the war it manufactured all types of military clothing. On Ministry of Supply contracts over 3 ½ million garments had been produced, amounting to a value of £2,000,000. After the war they produced demob suits and a full midday meal in the canteen cost only sixpence.

At work in the cutting room of Polikoff's clothing factory in Ynyswen in 1970 are, left to right: Danny Thomas; John Davies and Gwyn Williams.

Cymmer Colliery, Porth, *c.* 1919.

Lewis Merthyr Colliery, Porth, *c.* 1904.

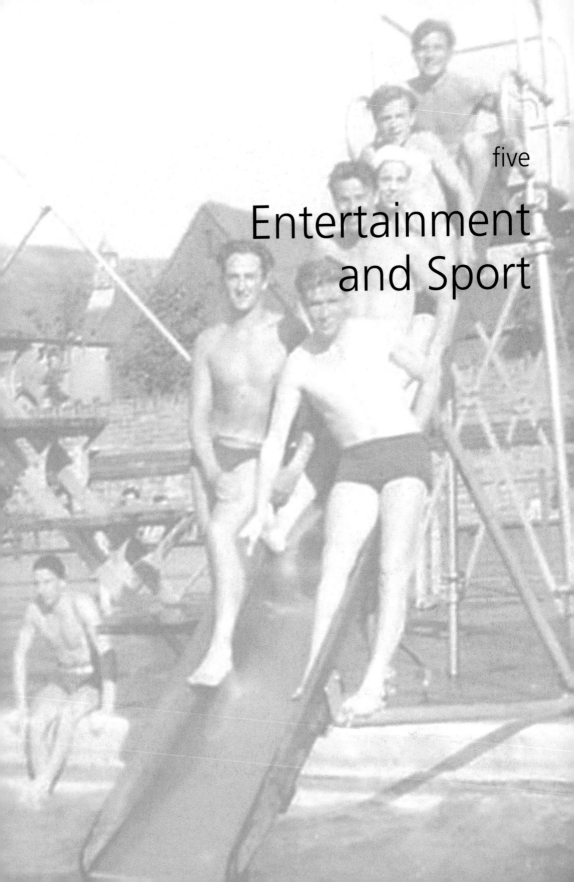

five

Entertainment and Sport

The Abergorki tug-of-war team.

Blaencwm Terrace, Tynewydd, celebrations for Queen Elizabeth's Coronation in 1953. From left to right, back row: Mrs Davies (Weston), -?-, Ivy Pritchard, Sylvia Sampson, Edna Smith, Gwyneth Jones, Ethel Rees, Brenda Rees, Maggie Davies, Doris Jones, Sarah Evans, -?- ,-?-, Glenys Davies, Gary Jones, Bess Rees, Margaret Davies and John Rees. Second row: Mrs Cook, Mrs Williams, Esther Cook, Marie Gwen Williams, Mary Ann Goodman, Mrs Cousins, Hilary Waters, -?-, John Sampson, -?-, -?-, Keith Doughty, Terry Williams, Keith Williams, -?-, -?-, Myra Doughty, Margaret Jones, -?- and Violet Rose. Third row: Margaret Evans, Jill Doughty, Margaret Sampson, -?-, Jeanette Sampson, Pat Smith, Beryl Cook, -?-, -?-, -?-, Mavis Davies, -?-, -?- and -?-. Fourth row: Marion Hudson, Leslie Hudson, -?-, Georgina Sampson, -?-, -?-, -?-, -?-, Gerald Rose and five unknowns. Front row: -?-, Jeffrey Sampson and Gerwyn Evans (standing).

Rhondda Boys Club's under-14 soccer team. From left to right, back row: -?-, -?-, -?-, Gareth ?, -?-, -?-, -?-, Jeff Green, Albert Nicholas, Albert Curtiss and Rhys Morgan Rees. Seated: Phillip Rees, Emrys Evans, -?-, Alan Curtiss, Phillip Lane and Jimmy Reynolds.

Blaenrhondda football team, 1950. Standing, left to right: Danny Morris, William (Fudgy) Lewis, Trevor Lewis, Idris Owen, Dixie Adams, Doug Richards, Glyn Parry and Dixie Lewis. Sitting: Will Wallace, Dai Waters, Gwyn Squires, Teddy Edwards, Glyn Davies and Reg Evans (Butch). In front are Ron Davies and Wally Pearce.

Fernhill Colliery workmen's bowling team, 1944. From left to right, back row: Harry Powell, 'Tiff' Davies, Tom Worral, Em Worral, ? Davies and -?-. Second row: Trevor Price, Alf Brown, -?-, Trevor Binding, Dil Adams, -?-, Danny Morris. Third row: -?-, Evan Ellis, -?-, Cyril Bishop, -?-, Elwyn Davies and -?-. Front row: Ken Morgan, Will Jenkins, Eufryn Bowen, John Lazarus, Jack Spurrey, 'Emo' Lewis, Mansel Williams and Dil Lee.

Treherbert Opera House Orchestra, *c.* 1910. The double bass player is Will Griffiths.

Members of Treherbert Amateur Operatic Society performing HMS *Pinafore* in Treherbert Opera House, February 1912.

Park and Dare Band, 1900–01.

Parc and Dare Band at Ystradfechan, 1923-24. Included in the photograph are Rhys Emrys Watkins (secretary), Emrys Brown, Edwin Watkins, Stan Bebb, Tom Evans, Emlyn Morgan, Will Williams, Trevor Williams, Ted Evans, Rufus Jones (conductor), Griff Higgon and Lewis Brown.

Parc and Dare Band, *c.* 1950. From left to right, back row: John Pearce, Lewis Brown, Derek Holvey, Ernie Coombes, Gwyn Jones, ? Thomas, George Morris, Dennis Coombes and Gordon Eddy. Second row: -?-, Don Humphries, Cyril Coombes, Berys Millward, Emlyn Morgan, Meirion Owen, Ieuan Morgan, Ivor Thomas and Harry Nutall (conductor). Front row: Griff Higgon, Cieron Thomas, Ivor Owen and Will Williams.

Members of Bethany Chapel, Treherbert, who performed in *Sir Roger De Colovere*, Treherbert Opera House are seen here around 1930. Back row, fifth from left, is Percy Evans.

Members of the Selsig Operatic Society, who performed in Straus's *Night in Venice* are seen here in 1981. From left to right: Stella Willey, Myra Thomas, Ann Holmes, Jill Evans and Aldyth Jones.

Members of the Selsig Operatic Society who performed in *The Gondoliers* in June 1966. From left to right: Tom Phelps, Myra Thomas, Will Thomas, Berl Jones and Eifion Evans.

Trevor Morte (front row, centre) Fernhill Colliery Agent Manager with Spanish competitors in the Gordon–Bennett International balloon race after their landing on 18 September 1921.

Treherbert Railway Canteen dance band, *c.* 1960. From left to right: Percy Beynon, ? Corey, Will Evans, Hugo Jones MC (in top hat), Danny Evans and Percy ?. The band was colloquially called 'The Silicosis Five' and the canteen 'The Casbah'. Hugo lost a leg working in the colliery and had an artifical leg fitted; the girls claimed he was a fantastic dancer.

Naval Officers' Jazz Band, Rhondda Fair, 5 June 1975. From left to right, back row: Pam Everett, Jean Legget, Rosemarie Morgan, Susan Everett, Lynette Sealey, Patti Jones, Caren Williams, Suzanne Jones, Sian Walters, Paula Rissoli, Susan Legget, Janeen Bradley, Sandra Bundock, Julie Davies, Rhiannon Minton, Jeline Davies, Lynda Merry, Anetta Groves, Julie Everett and Carol Best. Front row, drummers: Jeffrey Ferguson, Anthony Hopton, Stephen Ferguson, Mervyn Davies, Robert Yeoman, Derek Jones, Steven Ferguson and Stephen Jones.

Treherbert Bowls Team at Blaenrhondda Bowling Green, c. 1985. From left to right, back row: Don Tegan, Mal Thomas, Don Jones, Glyn Owen, Mal Squires, Mal Merrit. Middle row: Len John, Dilwyn Morgan, Arthur Jones, Gary ?, Ron Coleman, Tom Parry and Bill Roberts. Front row: George Palmer, Stan King and Cyril John.

Treherbert Swimming Pool Team 1960. From left to right, back row: Nigel Mortimer, Beezer Davies, Derek Dando, Colin Price. Bleddyn Eynon (in front of Colin Price), Derek Spear, Rhydian Daniels and Ricky Benbow. Second row: Don Williams, Arthur Davies, -?-, Helen Williams, -?-, -?-, -?-, Carol Griffiths, -?-, Carol Smith, -?- and Mr Butler. Third row: -?-, -?-, Lynn Jones, -?-, Terry Jones, ? Jenkins, Mr Thomas (baths' superintendant), Gordon Bozanko, Merryl Price, -?-, Blod Jones and -?-. Front row: Huw Davies, -?-, Alan Lewis, Dennis Jones,-?-, ? Warren, -?-, -?-, -?-.

Opposite above: Swimmers on the chute at Treherbert Swimming Pool, *c.* 1955. From bottom to top are: Gwynfor Evans (on the right), Don Squires, Cyril Lewis, Dilys Evans, Elwyn Davies and Ryland Marshal.

Opposite below left: Bute Dam, Cwmsaebren basin, Treherbert, *c.* 1932. As there were no swimming pools at the top end of the valley, people would use the disused colliery feeders or mountain streams for swimming.

Opposite below right: Members of the Treherbert Town football team, 1948. From left to right: George Fisher, Charlie Fisher and Les Richards.

Treorchy RFC match against Glam Police, season 1947/48. From left to right, back row: D. Evans, C. Evans, H. Nichols and A. Morris. Second row: A. Croster, H. Bowen, G. Richards, K. Dorrington, W.B. Cleaver, G. Hopkins, R. Wynne, M. Broom, J. Rees and D. Daniels. Front row: M. Jenkins, C. Whittingham, R. Richards, D. James (captain), E. Evans (secretary), E. Thomas, D. Fitzpatrick and J. Phillips.

Blaenrhondda Youth Club rounders team, 1952. From left to right, back row: Tom Jones, Mavis Williams, Marion Lewis, Margaret Evans and Harry Corfield. Second row: Glesni Jones, Sylvia Watts, -?- and -?-. Front row: Elizabeth Davies and -?-.

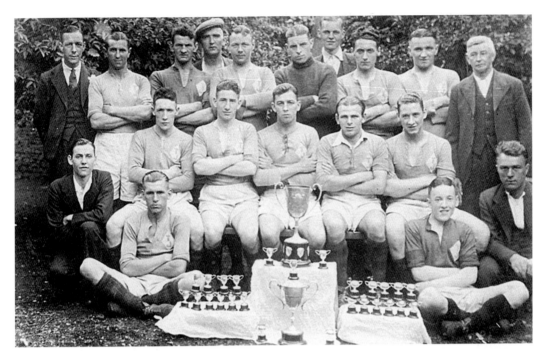

Treherbert Juniors football team 1933/34. From left to right, back row: -?-, -?-, -?-, Dai Morris, Eddy Gough, Cyril John, ? Smart, -?-, -?- and Dai Sheridan. Sitting: Glyn Davies, Danny Fitzgerald, -?-, Will Jenkins and ? Greedy. Front row: Charlie Thomas, Ben Rees, John Pearce and Will Longhurst.

Tydraw Colliery Male Choir, c. 1930. From left to right, back row: William Henry Evans, ? Davies, Trevor Evans, I. Rees, George Evans, Dai Hopkins, ? Pratt, William Rees, Haydn Kinsey and Fynlais Davies. Middle row: Dai Roderick Evans, Emlyn Jones, Glyn Davies, Tom Broome, Morlais Evans, Glyn Lisle, Fred Woods, Tom Richards and Will Jones. Front row: Emrys Thomas, Ivor Watts, Sam Lazarus, Tom Harris, Dai Griffiths, Walt Murray, Owen Evans, Dai John Williams and Sam Nicholas.

Carmel Chapel Concert Ali Baba, 1950. From left to right: Keith Greedy, Maralyn Morris, Carol Owen, Gaynor Richards, Jean Fisher, Owen Jenkins, Diane Morris, Carol Morris and Alun Jenkins.

Tynewydd Ladies Choir, c. 1935. From left to right, back row: Mrs Jones (Swansea), Ethel Lazarus, May Jones, Mrs Squires, Myra Abraham, Annie May Jones, Mrs Bowen, -?-, -?-. Second row: Mrs Jones (The Don), Mrs Pratt, Mrs Williams, Mrs Kinsey, -?-, Mrs White, Mrs Williams, Olwen Hopkins, Blodwen Harris, Mrs Bowen, Gwyneth Jones. Sitting: Mrs Edmunds, -?-, Ben Jones, Lizzie Joyce Davies, Mr Price, Glenys Farnham, David James Nicholas, Lil Edwards, Mrs Williams. Front row: Nan Mason, ? Roderick, Dai Davies (The Kick), Annie May Edwards, Mrs Bowen. The choir practiced twice a week in the billiard room of the Tydraw Institute.

Parc and Dare Band at the Daily Herald contest in the Albert Hall 1945 when the band took third place. From left to right, back row: Berys Millward, Lewis Brown, Will Davies, Gwilym Hunt, Ernie Coombes, Griff Higgon, Trevor Evans, Gwyn Jones and Rhys Emrys Watkins. Second row: Jack Smith, Ron Baker, Will Williams, Tom Atkins, Eric Davies, Evan Richards, Jack Coombes, Harry Nutall, Heron Trotman and Ieuan Watkins. Front row: Cliff Edmunds, Fred Prior, Emrys Brown, Haydn Bebb (conductor), Peter Durant, Emlyn Morgan, Arthur Jones, Cyril Coombes.

THE BOYS' CLUBS OF WALES

Chairman:	*President:*	*Hon. Treasurer:*
D. E. J. DAVIES, B.A., LL.B.	SIR MAYNARD JENOUR,	P. F. GILLAM,
General Secretary:	T.D., J.P., V.L.	**26 HIGH STREET**
G. H. STOKES, M.B.E.		**CARDIFF**
Appeals Organiser and		**CF1 2RR**
Sports Adviser:		*Telephone:*
CLIVE THOMAS		CARDIFF 36249 36240
Field Officer:		
S. JAMES-ROBERTSON		

OUR REFERENCE: CT/GH/S/AP

YOUR REFERENCE:

18th. April 1969.

Dear Haydn,

Please find enclosed photographs
taken during Frankie Vaughan's visit to
the Treherbert Boys' Club in October last,
and which you might like to keep as a
momento of the visit, with my compliments.

Best wishes,
Yours sincerely,

Clive Thomas
Sports Adviser and AppealOrganiser

Mr. H. Bundock,
4 Scott Street,
TREHERBERT,
Glam.

Letter from Clive Thomas (World Cup referee) to Haydn Bundock, president of the Treherbert Boys'
Club, enclosing photographs taken during the visit by Frankie Vaughan to the club in October 1969.
Clive Thomas refereed Brazil *vs* Sweden in the 1978 World Cup. He blew the final whistle while
a corner was being taken by Brazil and the subsequent goal scored was disallowed, thus creating
worldwide controversy.

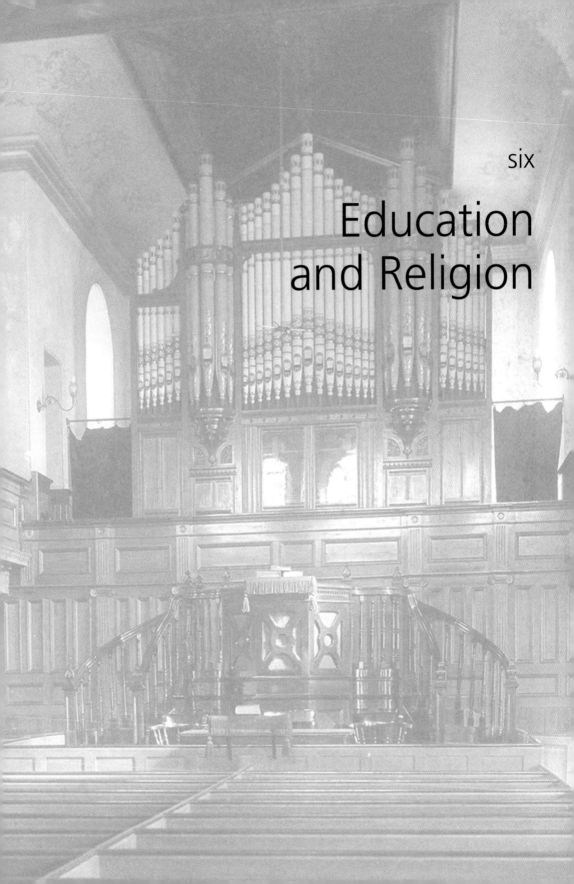

six

Education
and Religion

Members of the Catholic Church of the Immaculate Conception, Treorchy in the late 1950s. From left to right, back row: Joe Cavalli, John Balestrazzi and Gareth Watkins. Front row: Joe Beynon, Cam Strinatti, Johnny Quirk and Dennis Davies.

Members of the Catholic church, Treorchy, *c.* 1952. From left to right: Jimmy Brennan, Stan Jones, Rene Basini, Canon Crawley, -?-, -?-, ? Snooks, A. Cavalli, John Wheeler, -?- and A. Sidoli.

The Catholic church, Treorchy. Members at the St Patrick's dance at the Pentre Legion Club (the Shack) from around 1956. From left to right back row: Ivor Davies, Eddy Quirk, Peter Handley and Dudley Morgan. Middle row: Sally Davies, Johnny Quirk, Phil O'Rourke, Teresa Morgan and Dennis Davies. Front row: Glenys Quirk, Pat Handley and Mr Cavalli.

Children in the May procession, 1956 at the Catholic Church of the Immaculate Conception, Treorchy. In the photograph are: Anthony Davies, Adriana Rabbiotti, Peter Davies, Elena Carpanini, Christine Davies, Stephen Hayes, Ruth Williams, Mary Strinatti, Giovanni Brachi, Susan Davies, Theresa Davies and Sandra Rabbiotti.

Parc Boys' School, Form 2, 1936. From left to right, back row: Tom Jones, Tommy Mackey, Johnny Breeze,-?-, Ossie Holmes, Billy Field and ? Price. Second row: Ernie Oliver (teacher), Arthur Searle, -?-, Stan James, -?-, ? Bevan, Alfie Cox, Eddy Davies and D.R. Rees (headmaster). Third row: ? Rowlands, Stanley Adams, -?-, David Price, -?-, David Watkins and Stanley Bevan. Front row: Handel Bevan, -?-, Tommy Thomas, Eddie Roberts and Alfie Thomas.

Cwmparc School, Group 2B, Class 1, 1902.

Treherbert Boys School, Form 1B, 1960. From left to right, back row: John Evans, Mike Green, Graham Drew, David Bassett, Keith Greedy, Gerald Thomas, Lynn Williams and -?-. Middle row: John Davies, Randal Wilkins, Gwyn Jones, Rob Penhale, Dennis Morgan, Peter Arundell, Lynn Rees and -?-. Front row: Clive Sheppard, Jeffrey Bayliss, Stuart Hill, David Ffoulkes, Cyril Hosking, Ray Bethel, Roger Jenkins and Trevor Daniel.

Treherbert Boys School, Form 3B, 1960. From left to right, back row: Gwyn Taylor, William Benton, Derek Dando, Keith Williams, Brian Green, Michael Thomas and William Evans. Middle row: David Pritchard, Brian Jones, Lynn Evans, Melville Morgan, Neil Owen, Gwilym Davies, Michael Thompson. Front row: M Sullivan and Vernon Evans.

Park Girls' School, Standard 3A, 1931.

Staff of Park School, Cwmparc, *c.* 1908.

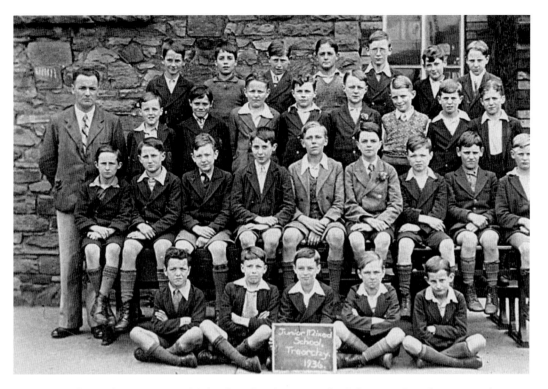

Boys of Treorchy Junior Mixed School. In the photo are: John Balestrazzi, Douglas Brunt and Howard ?.

Porth Secondary School woodwork class, *c.* 1928.

Carmel Chapel, Penyrenglyn, *c.* 1912.

Interior of Carmel Chapel, Penyrenglyn, *c*. 1912.

Graigddu School, Dinas, *c.* 1900.

Teachers and staff of Graigddu School, Dinas, *c.* 1900.

Porth Higher Grade and PTC football team 1914/15.

Form 3A Porth Secondary School, *c.* 1928. Back row, fourth from the right is Ossie Morgan who became a well-known teacher and rugby referee.

Siloh Chapel, Llewellyn Street, Pentre, *c.* 1904.

Members of Siloh Chapel, Pentre, *c.* 1970. Back row, centre is Minister Emrys Jones and in the front row are the chapel deacons.

Treherbert Boys School, *c.* 1928. Front row centre is headmaster Mr W.J. Jones also in the photograph is Mr Tom Duggan, Mr Percy Brokenbrow, Mr W.J. Gruar, Mr Pearce, Mr Samuel Howells and Mr J.R. Edwards.

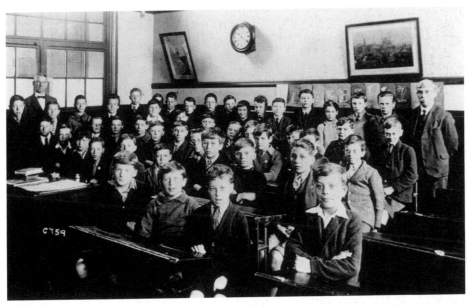

Treherbert Boys School 1927. Class Standard 7, in the back left is Mr S. Howells (teacher) on the right is Mr W.J. Jones (headmaster) among the boys are: H. Eldridge, Len Evans, S. Morris, David Rees, Les Curry, Mervyn Lloyd, Dilwyn Pugh, Haydn Griffiths, Trevor Thomas, John Jones, Bryn Thomas, Tommy Childs, Raymond Edwards, Jimmy Thomas, Ernie Hart, Ron Thomas, Trevor Gough, Jack Leason, Handel Williams, Cyril Bryant, Haydn Cassam, Arthur Davies, David Thomas, Leslie Jenkins, Ivor Purdell, Morgan Williams, Glyn Williams, Donald Walters, Emrys Owen and Nicholas Jones.

Treherbert Senior Boys School rugby team 1926/27. Standing on the left is Pyer Davies and on the right is Mr Davies (science). Sitting, left to right are: J.R. Edwards (teacher), Mr Jones (headmaster), and John Gruar (teacher).

seven

Townships

View of Pentre looking towards Treorchy from St Peter's church tower. Behind the line of washing is the vicarage and above that is Tynybedw Colliery. The 'Swamp' bridge can be seen crossing the main road onto the sidings behind Volunteer Street.

Clyngwyn, Blaenrhondda, *c.* 1950. Clyngwyn farm can be seen in the background and the houses in Blaenrhondda Road on the left and right are in the process of being built.

Bridgend Square, Ton Pentre from around 1930 after the erection of Belisha Beacons, named after the then Transport Minister, Hore Belisha.

Bute Street, Treorchy, *c.* 1945.

Heol Ceiriog, Wattstown, 22 June 1928.

Heol Y Twyn Road, Wattstown, 22 June 1928.

Bute Street, Treorchy, *c.* 1903.

Bute Street, Treorchy, *c.* 1920. On the right were: No. 83 Mrs Annie Cooke, fruiterer; No. 95 Evan Brunt, tobacconist; David Butler hairdresser; No. 99 National Provincial Bank; No. 100 Barclays Bank and on the left were: No. 103 David Williams, confectioners; No. 105, Thomas Davies, butcher, No. 106 Evan Jones and Co., drapers, and No. 107 George Oliver, shoe wharehouse.

Maendy Hill, Pentre, *c.* 1904.

Gelli Road Gelli, *c.* 1930. Gwyn Moses standing outside his draper shop at Nos 159–160. The lady standing in the doorway on the left is Kathleen Harris, shop assistant.

Bute Street from Cardiff Arms Square, Treorchy, *c.* 1945.

Cardiff Arms Square, Treorchy, *c.* 1906. Cardiff Arms hotel was the home of Treorchy RFC. The open space in front was used as a site for a mini-market on Saturday nights where Len Rose sold pickled onions.

Carne Street, Pentre, *c.* 1913. This photograph clearly shows the system, used by the Rhondda Tramways Co. Ltd, for trams to pass each other. The main line was a single track and the tram had a driving platform on both ends, so never needed to be turned around. The tram was driven into the loop and waited for the tram from the opposite direction to arrive. When it had passed, the cable boom was crossed over and the first tram proceeded on its way out of the loop.

Cemetery Road, Trealaw, *c.* 1904.

Church Road, Ton Pentre, *c.* 1900.

Church Road, Ton Pentre, 1902. On the right is the Maendy and Eastern Workman's Hall and Library, erected by the workmen of Maendy and Eastern Pits (Ocean collieries), which was opened in 1895 at a cost of £8,000. The hall, which was erected in 1900, is used as a picture and variety theatre. The Ton Industrial Co-operative Society Ltd is on the left.

Ton Pentre Police Station shortly after its erection in 1902.

Stag Square, Treorchy, *c.* 1903. On the left is Daniel Evans hairdresser at No. 13 High Street. The Stag Hotel is on the right. Note the gas lamp is in the middle of the road and the water spout on the left.

Penygraig Road, Penygraig, *c.* 1906. On the left is the Butchers Arms Hotel. Job Churchill, saddler and harness maker at No. 5 Penygraig Road, was trainer-manager to boxer Tommy Farr, who fought Joe Louis for the heavyweight championship of the world in 1937.

High Street, Treorchy, *c.* 1912. With Noddfa Chapel on the right.

Hannah Street, Porth, *c.* 1905.

Bute Street, Treherbert, c. 1940. During the war years one of the only professions allowed to drive cars were doctors, because of the shortage of petrol. The bicycle was the best means of transport.

Ynyshir Road, Lower end of Ynyshir, c. 1920. On the right is William Evans' draper's shop.

Dewinton Street, Tonypandy, *c.* 1906.

Bridge Street linking Tonypandy with Trealaw 23 February 1980. To the left in the photograph is the railway booking office and on the right is Tonypandy Central Hall.

Duffryn Street, Ferndale, *c.* 1912.

Ferndale Road, Tylorstown, *c.* 1913. On the left is the Fern Vale Brewery.

Dunraven Street, Tonypandy, *c.* 1902.

Dunraven Street, Tonypandy, *c.* 1905.

Hannah Street, Porth, *c.* 1900.

Maerdy Road, Maerdy, *c.* 1916.

Pandy Square, Tonypandy, *c.* 1940. On the left is the Pandy Hotel, a part of the Picturedrome cinema's roof can also be seen and the Thistle Hotel is next to the van. The large building next door is the Co-operative and South Wales Furnishers.

Picturedrome cinema, Tonypandy was used as a bingo hall before final closure.

Porth Cottage Hospital was erected in 1895 at a cost of £3,600, and enlarged in 1908. It contained five wards of thirty-three beds.

Porth Square, *c.* 1937. Seen here from Cymmer Hill, with the infamous urinal in the centre of the square.

Ystrad Road, Pentre, *c.* 1906. On the left is A. Cule & Sons, drapers who occupied three premises. On the right is the National Provincial and Union Bank of England Ltd.

Ystrad Road, Pentre, *c.* 1913. From left to right: No. 194 Edith Ladd, jeweller and silversmith; No. 195 Briggs and Co., boot and shoe maker; No. 196 Price and Co., grocer with the Popular Hotel situated on the second and third floors; No. 197 Miss Sarah Rees Smith, draper, No. 198 Kate McKintosh, fancy draper and No. 199 Maypole Dairy Co. Ltd, provisions. Note the winged griffins on the roof crests.

View of Cwmdare, Cwmparc.

Lower Cwmparc, *c.* 1930. The hexagonal building was used by the Park and Dare Silver band when they wanted to practice.

Treherbert and Penyrenglyn, *c.* 1920. In front is the Rhondda Valley Brewery Co. Ltd, Penyrenglyn School is in the background with Ynysofeio Avenue and Herbert Street (colloquially known as 'The Town') and to the right, the two pit head gears of Ynysofei Top Colliery. The white buildings in front of the school are River Row.

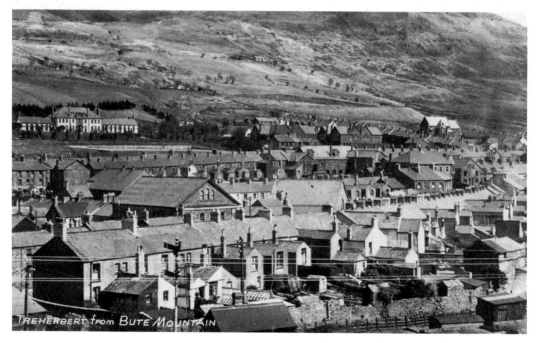

Treherbert viewed from Bute Mountain, *c.* 1940.

Partridge Road, Llwynypia, *c.* 1938. On the right is the bus shelter next to the entrance to the hospital.

Ystrad Road, Pentre, *c.* 1917. To the left in this photograph, at No. 1, is William Lock, butcher and behind the lorry is the Woodfield Hotel. On the right is No. 221 Albion House and No. 224 John Archibald Harries, hairdresser and next door, another butcher's shop. Note the meat hanging outside the butchers' shops and bear in mind that at the rear of the shop's right-hand side was Pentre Colliery with all the dust and small coal.

Llewellyn Street, Pentre, *c.* 1906.

An unknown Rhondda family from Cwmparc pose for their portrait. They were typical of the hard-working families to be found in this area at the turn of the nineteenth century.

Other local titles published by Tempus

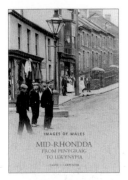

Mid-Rhondda: From Penygraig to Llwynypia
DAVID J. CARPENTER

Once a sparsely-populated area, the Rhondda Valley became heavily industrialised with the arrival of coal mining. Some 150 years later however, the mines are closed and the recession stole away the livelihoods of many. A fighting spirit in hard times is now remembered as a brighter, greener future approaches. With over 180 archive images this pictorial history charts the rise and fall of the industrial society of Tonypandy, Penygraig, Trealaw, Clydach Vale and Llwynypia.

07524 3210 9

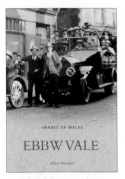

Ebbw Vale
IDWAL WILLIAMS

Ebbw Vale's strong industrial history is well represented in this comprehensive collection of nearly 200 archive images, some of which date from as early as the 1900s. This book recalls life as it once was before the huge loss of steel industry jobs, and depicts the history of this part of Gwent in terms of its society, its culture and its industry.

07524 3209 5

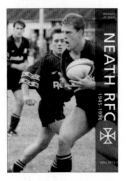

Neath RFC 1945–1996
MIKE PRICE

Neath Rugby Football Club is the oldest senior club in Wales and the Welsh All Blacks have enjoyed a long and proud history. This is the second Images of Sport volume devoted to the development of Neath RFC and it covers the period from 1945 to 1996 – from the end of the Second World War to professionalism.

07524 3106 4

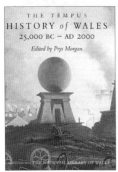

The Tempus History of Wales
PRYS MORGAN

Wales was at the heart of the Industrial Revolution, towns like Merthyr Tidfil driving the engine of the British Empire. The cultural and social divide between modern, industrialised Wales and the traditional agricultural areas is explored within this comprehensive volume.

07524 1983 8

If you are interested in purchasing other books published by Tempus, or in case you have difficulty finding any Tempus books in your local bookshop, you can also place orders directly through our website

www.tempus-publishing.com